Seeds of Change: A Journey to Ramsey

The Impact Chronicles, Volume 1

Paul Smith

Published by Paul Smith, 2024.

SEEDS OF CHANGE: A JOURNEY TO RAMSEY

First edition. February 23, 2024.

ISBN: 979-8224647842

Written by Paul Smith.

Table of Contents

To my Late Father who had Parkinson's - Mr Malcolm Smith 1949-2020 whom Grand Chrildren now live on the island.

Book 1
Series Title: The Impact Chronicles

Synopsis:

"The Impact Chronicles" is a series of interconnected stories that celebrates the

resilience, courage, and compassion of individuals striving to make a difference in

their communities and the world at large. Each instalment follows the journeys of

diverse characters as they navigate personal challenges, overcome obstacles, and

discover the transformative power of collective action.

Book 1
Title: Seeds of Change: A Journey to Ramsey

In Summary:

In the first instalment of the "Seeds of Change" series, we follow the interconnected

stories of four individuals – Maria, David, Emily, and Adam – as they embark on a

journey to the coastal town of Ramsey in search of new beginnings.

Maria, a seasoned activist, arrives in Ramsey with a vision of creating community

gardens to promote food security and social cohesion. David, an environmental engineer, sees Ramsey as an opportunity to implement green infrastructure projects

that will mitigate the effects of climate change and enhance the town's resilience.

Emily, a digital influencer, finds herself drawn to Ramsey's picturesque landscapes

and vibrant community spirit. With her online platform, she seeks to raise awareness

about local issues and inspire others to take action.

Adam, a marine biologist, is captivated by Ramsey's rich marine biodiversity and

sees potential in establishing a sea life sanctuary and tropical aquarium to educate

and engage visitors.

As these four individuals settle into Ramsey, they encounter challenges and setbacks

but also discover the power of community, resilience, and hope. Together, they plant

the seeds of change that will transform Ramsey into a beacon of sustainability,

compassion, and renewal.

Through their journeys of self-discovery and collective action, Maria, David, Emily,

and Adam demonstrate that even in the face of adversity, ordinary individuals can

make an extraordinary impact when they come together with a shared purpose.

Let's go way back to the beginning all those years ago.

Chapter 1: A New Dawn

The first light of dawn crept through the curtains, casting a soft glow upon Emily's

face as she stirred from her slumber. She blinked sleepily, stretching her limbs as she

welcomed the new day. With a sense of anticipation tingling in her veins, she rose

from her bed and made her way to the window.

Pulling back the curtains, Emily was greeted by the sight of the sun rising over the

sleepy town of Ramsey. Its golden rays painted the sky with hues of pink and orange,

illuminating the cobblestone streets below. The town was just beginning to stir, its

inhabitants awakening to the promise of a fresh start.

Emily smiled as she took in the scene before her. It was a new day, filled with endless

possibilities, and she couldn't help but feel a sense of excitement bubbling up inside

her. With a determined spring in her step, she set about her morning routine, eager to

seize the day and make the most of every moment.

As she prepared breakfast in her cosy kitchen, Emily's thoughts drifted to the challenges and opportunities that lay ahead. She had big dreams and aspirations,

and she knew that today was the first step towards turning them into reality. With a

deep breath and a heart full of hope, she embraced the dawn of a new day and all the

possibilities it held.

Little did she know, her life was about to intersect with those of others in ways she

could never have imagined. In the heart of the city, Maria was already hard at work,

determined to provide for her family despite the odds stacked against her. Across

town, David tended to his urban garden with care and dedication, finding solace and

purpose amidst the concrete jungle.

And so, as the sun continued its ascent into the sky, casting its warm light upon the

town of Ramsey, the stage was set for a series of encounters that would change the

lives of Emily and her fellow inhabitants forever. For in this new dawn, anything was

possible, and the seeds of change were just beginning to take root.

Chapter 2: Maria's Dream

In the heart of Ramsey, where the cobblestone streets echoed with the rhythm of

daily life, Maria rose before the sun. With a tired but determined spirit, she greeted

the day with a sense of purpose that belied the challenges she faced.

As Maria prepared breakfast for her children in their small apartment, her thoughts

drifted to the dream that had sustained her through the darkest of times. It was a

dream of hope and possibility, a dream of breaking free from the cycle of poverty

that had held her family captive for generations.

With her youngest child clinging to her apron strings, Maria stole a moment to

herself, closing her eyes and envisioning a better future. In her mind's eye, she saw a

bustling marketplace filled with fresh produce and vibrant colours, a place where her

homemade tamales and tortillas would be the talk of the town.

But the road to realising her dream was fraught with obstacles. Money was tight, and

every penny earned from her job as a waitress at the local diner went towards putting

food on the table and keeping a roof over their heads. There were days when it felt
like the weight of the world was on her shoulders, and she wondered if she would
ever be able to break free from the cycle of poverty that had plagued her family for
generations.

But Maria was not one to give up easily. With a steely resolve and a heart full of
determination, she set out to make her dream a reality. She saved every spare dime,
cutting back on expenses wherever she could, and squirrelling away whatever she
could spare.

And then, one day, opportunity came knocking at her door. A small storefront
became available in the heart of town, and Maria saw her chance to turn her dream
into a reality. With trembling hands and a heart full of hope, she signed the lease and
set to work transforming the space into her vision of a bustling marketplace.

As the sun rose higher in the sky, casting its warm light upon the streets of Ramsey,
Maria's dream began to take shape. With each passing day, the storefront became
more than just a building—it became a beacon of hope and possibility for the entire
community.

And as Maria stood in the doorway of her new marketplace, watching as customers streamed in to sample her delicious homemade fare, she knew that her dream had

finally come true. For in that moment, she realised that with hard work,

Chapter 3: David's Garden

In the heart of the bustling city, amidst the concrete and steel, David found solace in

the simple act of gardening. For him, the urban jungle was not a place of chaos and

noise, but rather a canvas upon which he could cultivate beauty and life.

With calloused hands and a heart full of determination, David tended to his garden

with care and dedication. In the small plot of land behind his apartment building, he

had created a verdant oasis amidst the urban sprawl—a place where flowers

bloomed, and vegetables thrived, despite the odds.

As the sun rose over the city skyline, casting its warm light upon the world below,

David set to work, his hands moving deftly as he tended to his plants. With each seed

he planted, each flower he nurtured, he felt a sense of peace wash over him—a

reminder that even in the midst of chaos, there was beauty to be found.

But David's garden was more than just a place of beauty—it was also a source of sustenance for him and his neighbours. As he harvested ripe tomatoes and crisp

lettuce, he shared the bounty of his garden with those in need, knowing that in times

of hardship, a fresh meal could make all the difference.

But David's garden was not just about feeding the body—it was also about feeding

the soul. For him, gardening was a form of therapy, a way to escape the stresses of

everyday life and reconnect with the earth. As he dug his hands into the soil, he felt a

sense of grounding, a reminder of his place in the world and the importance of

nurturing life in all its forms.

And so, as the sun dipped below the horizon, casting long shadows across the city

streets, David stood amidst his garden, a smile playing at the corners of his lips. For

in that moment, he knew that no matter what challenges lay ahead, he would always

find peace and purpose in the simple act of gardening.

determination, and a little bit of luck, anything was possible.

Chapter 4: Emily's Resolve

As Emily settles into her new life in Ramsey, she finds herself grappling with

uncertainty and doubt. The quaint coastal town is a far cry from the bustling city she

once called home, and she wonders if she made the right decision to uproot her life

for a fresh start.

Despite her initial hesitations, Emily's resolve is unwavering. With each passing day,

she immerses herself in the vibrant community of Ramsey, eager to make a

meaningful impact. Drawing upon her skills as a digital influencer, Emily begins to

document her experiences and share stories of the town's charm and character with

her online followers.

As she explores Ramsey's hidden gems and connects with local residents, Emily

discovers a sense of purpose and belonging she never thought possible. From

supporting small businesses to volunteering at community events, she throws herself into every opportunity to contribute to Ramsey's growth and prosperity.

But Emily's journey is not without its challenges. As she navigates the complexities

of small-town life, she encounters resistance and scepticism from some residents

who are wary of outsiders. Undeterred, Emily remains steadfast in her commitment

to building bridges and fostering understanding, determined to prove that

newcomers like her can be valuable assets to the community.

With each obstacle she faces, Emily's resolve only strengthens. Armed with

optimism, empathy, and a willingness to learn, she embraces the opportunity to be a

catalyst for positive change in Ramsey, determined to sow the seeds of hope and

resilience that will flourish for years to come.

Chapter 5: Adam's Passion

As the days pass in Ramsey, Adam's passion for marine life grows stronger with

each passing moment. He spends hours exploring the rocky shores and sandy

beaches, marvelling at the diverse array of creatures that call the ocean home.

But it's not just the beauty of the sea that captivates Adam—it's the delicate balance

of life beneath the waves, and the urgent need to protect and preserve it for future

generations. Inspired by his love for the ocean, Adam begins to envision a way to

share his passion with others and make a positive impact on the world around him.

With Emily's unwavering support, Adam starts to research ways to turn his dream

into reality. He spends countless hours poring over books and articles, soaking up

knowledge about marine biology, conservation, and sustainable living.

As he delves deeper into his studies, Adam begins to see the potential for creating something truly special—a sea life sanctuary and tropical aquarium that could not

only educate and inspire visitors but also help support the local economy and

promote environmental stewardship.

With his vision taking shape, Adam shares his ideas with Emily and their friends,

Maria and David. Together, they brainstorm ways to bring the project to life, pooling

their resources and expertise to overcome any obstacles that stand in their way.

As they work tirelessly to turn their dream into reality, Adam's passion for marine life

becomes a driving force behind their efforts. And as the days turn into weeks, and

the weeks into months, they come to realise that with enough determination and

dedication, anything is possible.

Chapter 6: Connecting Paths

As the sun rises over Ramsey's picturesque coastline, Maria, David, Emily, and

Adam find themselves drawn together by a shared sense of purpose and

possibility. Each of them brings their own unique strengths and passions to the

table, but it's their shared vision of creating positive change in their new

community that binds them together.

With the foundation of their friendship growing stronger each day, they begin to

explore ways to collaborate on projects that align with their individual interests

and talents. Maria's background in community organising proves invaluable as

she mobilises local residents to get involved in initiatives aimed at improving the

town's infrastructure and fostering a sense of belonging.

Meanwhile, David's expertise in horticulture inspires him to launch a community

garden project, bringing together neighbours of all ages to cultivate fresh produce and beautify public spaces. His enthusiasm is contagious, and soon the garden

becomes a vibrant hub of activity, with residents coming together to share

gardening tips, swap stories, and forge new connections.

Emily's passion for storytelling and digital media channels finds expression in her

efforts to document the town's transformation. Through captivating photographs

and heartfelt narratives, she shines a spotlight on the people and places that

make Ramsey such a special place to call home, inspiring others to join in the

journey of change.

And at the heart of it all is Adam, whose boundless enthusiasm for marine life

fuels his ambition to create a sea life sanctuary and tropical aquarium that will

not only educate and entertain visitors but also serve as a catalyst for environmental conservation and stewardship.

As they work together to bring their respective projects to fruition, Maria, David,

Emily, and Adam find themselves forging bonds that transcend friendship—they're

creating a true sense of community, where everyone has a role to play and every

voice is heard. And as they look to the future, they do so with hope and optimism,

knowing that together, they can make a difference in the world around them.

Chapter 7: Seeds of Compassion

As the winds of change continue to blow through Ramsey, Maria, David, Emily,

and Adam find themselves inspired by the resilience and compassion of their

fellow residents. Despite the challenges they face, the people of Ramsey come

together in times of need, offering support and solidarity to those who need it

most.

Moved by the spirit of their community, Maria and David organise a series of

volunteer events aimed at addressing pressing social issues, from food insecurity

to homelessness. Together with their neighbours, they roll up their sleeves and

get to work, making a tangible difference in the lives of those less fortunate.

Meanwhile, Emily channels her passion for storytelling into a series of blog posts

and social media campaigns aimed at raising awareness about local

environmental issues. Through her evocative writing and captivating

photographs, she shines a spotlight on the beauty of Ramsey's

natural

surroundings and the importance of preserving them for future generations.

And at the heart of it all is Adam, whose dream of creating a sea life sanctuary

and tropical aquarium takes on new meaning as he witnesses the impact of his

community's collective efforts. With each volunteer event and social media post,

he sees firsthand the power of compassion to bring about positive change in the

world.

As they work together to sow the seeds of compassion in their community, Maria,

David, Emily, and Adam find themselves drawn closer together than ever before.

Their shared values and common goals unite them in a common purpose, as they

strive to create a better, more compassionate world for themselves and future

generations. And as they look to the future, they do so with hope in their hearts

and a renewed sense of purpose, knowing that their collective efforts can truly

make a difference.

Chapter 8: Cultivating Change

With the seeds of compassion firmly planted, Maria, David, Emily, and Adam set

their sights on cultivating lasting change in their community. Drawing on their

collective strengths and passions, they embark on a series of initiatives aimed at

addressing the root causes of social and environmental issues in Ramsey.

Maria takes the lead on organising a community-wide clean-up effort, rallying

residents to join forces in sprucing up public spaces and beautifying neglected

areas of the town. With brooms, rakes, and garbage bags in hand, volunteers of

all ages come together to clear away litter and debris, transforming Ramsey into

a cleaner, more inviting place to live.

Meanwhile, David's community garden project continues to flourish, providing a

source of fresh, nutritious food for local families and fostering a sense of

connection among neighbours. With each harvest, the garden becomes a symbol of resilience and self-sufficiency, demonstrating the power of community-led

initiatives to address food insecurity and promote healthy living.

Emily's storytelling efforts take on new significance as she turns her attention to

documenting the impact of their collective efforts on the town. Through a series

of multimedia presentations and online campaigns, she shares stories of

resilience, hope, and positive change, inspiring others to get involved and make a

difference in their own communities.

And at the heart of it all is Adam, whose vision for a sea life sanctuary and

tropical aquarium continues to take shape. With the support of his friends and

neighbours, he secures funding and resources to bring his dream to life,

transforming an abandoned building into a vibrant hub of marine education and

conservation.

As they work together to cultivate change in Ramsey, Maria, David, Emily, and

Adam find themselves inspired by the resilience and generosity of their

community. With each project they undertake, they see firsthand the

transformative power of collective action and the profound impact it can have on

the lives of those around them. And as they look to the future, they do so with a

renewed sense of purpose and determination, knowing that together, they can create a brighter, more sustainable future for Ramsey and beyond.

Chapter 9: Challenges and Triumphs

As Maria, David, Emily, and Adam continue their journey of community building in

Ramsey, they encounter both challenges and triumphs along the way. Despite

their best efforts, they face setbacks and obstacles that put their resolve to the

test. Yet, through perseverance and determination, they find ways to overcome

adversity and emerge stronger than ever.

One of their biggest challenges arises when funding for Adam's sea life sanctuary

project falls through, leaving them scrambling to find alternative sources of

support. Undeterred, they launch a crowdfunding campaign and reach out to local

businesses and philanthropic organisations for sponsorship, eventually securing

the resources they need to move forward with the project.

Meanwhile, David's community garden faces its own set of challenges, including

inclement weather and pest infestations that threaten to derail the harvest. But with the help of dedicated volunteers and innovative gardening techniques,

they're able to overcome these obstacles and enjoy a bountiful crop that feeds

dozens of families in need.

Emily's storytelling efforts also hit a snag when her computer crashes, causing

her to lose months' worth of photographs and writing. Devastated but undeterred,

she enlists the help of her friends to recreate her lost work and redouble her

efforts to document the positive changes taking place in Ramsey.

Through it all, Maria serves as a pillar of strength and support for her friends,

offering words of encouragement and practical assistance whenever they need it

most. Together, they weather the storms of adversity and celebrate the triumphs

of their collective efforts, knowing that every challenge they overcome brings

them one step closer to their shared vision of a better, more resilient Ramsey.

As they reflect on their journey so far, Maria, David, Emily, and Adam are filled with

a sense of pride and accomplishment. They've faced their fair share of obstacles

along the way, but they've also experienced moments of joy, camaraderie, and

shared purpose that have brought them closer together as friends and

collaborators. And as they look to the future, they do so with renewed determination and optimism, knowing that whatever challenges lie ahead, they'll

face them together, as a community united in their commitment to positive

Change.

Chapter 10: Bonds of Friendship

In the heart of Ramsey, amidst the hustle and bustle of their various projects, Maria,

David, Emily, and Adam find solace and strength in the bonds of friendship they've

forged. Through shared experiences, laughter, and tears, they discover the true value

of companionship and support, as they navigate the highs and lows of their journey

together.

As they work side by side on their respective initiatives, they share moments of joy

and celebration, whether it's harvesting fresh produce from David's community

garden, unveiling a new exhibit at Adam's sea life sanctuary, or watching Emily's

online storytelling efforts reach new audiences around the world. In each other's

company, they find inspiration and encouragement, fueling their passion for making a

difference in their community.

But it's not just the successes that bring them closer together; it's also the challenges they face along the way. When setbacks arise, they lean on each other for

guidance and support, offering words of encouragement and lending a helping hand

whenever needed. Through their shared experiences of triumph and adversity, they

deepen their bonds and solidify their commitment to each other and to the

community they've come to call home.

As they reflect on the journey they've undertaken together, Maria, David, Emily, and

Adam are grateful for the friendships they've formed and the support they've

received along the way. They know that no matter what the future holds, they'll

always have each other's backs, ready to face whatever challenges may come their

way with courage, resilience, and unwavering friendship. And as they look ahead to

the next chapter of their adventure, they do so with hearts full of gratitude and

optimism, knowing that with their friends by their side, anything is possible.

Chapter 11: Overcoming Adversity

As Maria, David, Emily, and Adam continue their journey of community-building in

Ramsey, they encounter a series of unforeseen challenges that put their resolve to

the test. From financial setbacks to logistical hurdles, they find themselves facing

obstacles that threaten to derail their efforts and dampen their spirits.

One of the biggest challenges they face is a sudden downturn in tourism, which has

a significant impact on the revenue streams for Adam's sea life sanctuary and

Emily's online storytelling platform. With fewer visitors coming to Ramsey, they

struggle to generate the funds needed to keep their projects afloat, forcing them to

get creative in finding alternative sources of income.

Meanwhile, David's community garden faces its own share of challenges, including a

particularly harsh winter that damages crops and disrupts planting schedules.

Undeterred, David and his team of volunteers work tirelessly to salvage what they can and come up with innovative solutions to protect their crops from the elements.

As they navigate these obstacles, Maria serves as a source of strength and support

for her friends, offering words of encouragement and practical assistance to help

them stay focused and resilient in the face of adversity. Together, they weather the

storms of uncertainty and emerge stronger and more determined than ever to see

their vision for Ramsey comes to fruition.

Despite the setbacks they encounter, Maria, David, Emily, and Adam refuse to give up

on their dreams. Through their collective determination and unwavering belief in the

power of community, they find ways to overcome adversity and continue moving

forward, one step at a time. And as they confront each new challenge with courage

and resilience, they prove that with perseverance and teamwork, anything is possible.

Chapter 12: The Power of Community

In the face of adversity, Maria, David, Emily, and Adam discover the true strength of

the community they've built in Ramsey. As they confront challenges and setbacks,

they find solace and support in the bonds they've forged with their neighbours and

fellow activists, who rally around them in their time of need.

When Adam's sea life sanctuary faces a funding shortfall, the community comes

together to organise a series of fundraising events, from bake sales to charity

auctions, to help keep the project afloat. Their efforts pay off as donations pour in

from local businesses and residents, demonstrating the power of collective action in

times of crisis.

Meanwhile, Emily's online storytelling platform receives an outpouring of support

from fans and followers around the world, who contribute both financially and

creatively to help keep the project alive. Their encouragement and generosity serve as a reminder of the impact that a dedicated community can have in uplifting and

sustaining one another.

David's community garden also benefits from the collective efforts of volunteers and

supporters, who come together to lend their time and expertise to ensure the

success of the project. Through their hard work and dedication, they're able to

overcome the challenges posed by inclement weather and resource shortages,

harvesting a bountiful crop that nourishes the entire community.

As Maria, David, Emily, and Adam reflect on the outpouring of support they've

received from their community, they're filled with gratitude and admiration for the

strength and resilience of the people of Ramsey. They realise that their journey

towards positive change is not one they need to undertake alone, but rather one that

is enriched and sustained by the power of community. And as they continue to work

towards their shared vision for a better future, they do so with the knowledge that

together, they are capable of overcoming any obstacle that stands in their way.

Chapter 13: Lessons Learned

In the wake of their recent challenges, Maria, David, Emily, and Adam take a moment

to reflect on the lessons they've learned along their journey in Ramsey. As they look

back on their experiences, they gain valuable insights that will shape their future

endeavours and guides them in their quest for positive change.

One of the most important lessons they've learned is the importance of resilience in

the face of adversity. Despite facing numerous setbacks and obstacles, they've

remained steadfast in their commitment to their goals, refusing to be deterred by the

challenges they've encountered. Through perseverance and determination, they've

discovered that even the most daunting challenges can be overcome with time and

effort.

They've also learned the power of collaboration and community. In times of need,

they've been humbled by the outpouring of support they've received from their neighbours and fellow activists, who have rallied around them to offer assistance

and encouragement. They've come to understand that real change is not achieved in

isolation, but through the collective efforts of like-minded individuals working

together towards a common goal.

Additionally, they've gained a deeper appreciation for the importance of staying true

to their values and convictions, even in the face of opposition or criticism. As they've

encountered resistance to their ideas and initiatives, they've remained steadfast in

their belief in the power of positive change, trusting in their vision and remaining

committed to their principles.

As Maria, David, Emily, and Adam continue on their journey, they carry these lessons

with them, knowing that they will serve as guiding principles in their ongoing efforts

to make a difference in their community and beyond. And as they face whatever

challenges the future may hold, they do so with confidence and determination, armed

with the wisdom they've gained along the way.

Chapter 14: Planting Seeds of Hope

Amidst the trials and triumphs of their journey, Maria, David, Emily, and Adam find

themselves at a pivotal moment of hope and renewal in Ramsey. Inspired by the

lessons they've learned and the support of their community, they set out to sow the

seeds of positive change and cultivate a brighter future for all.

With renewed determination, they redouble their efforts to advance their projects and

initiatives, from Adam's sea life sanctuary to Emily's online storytelling platform.

They harness the momentum generated by their recent challenges to fuel their

progress, channelling their energy into making a lasting impact on their community.

As they work tirelessly to bring their vision to life, they begin to see the fruits of their

labour blossoms before their eyes. The sea life sanctuary attracts visitors from near

and far, providing an educational and immersive experience that fosters a deeper

appreciation for marine life and environmental conservation. Meanwhile, Emily's online storytelling platform continues to reach new audiences and inspire positive

change through the power of storytelling and advocacy.

But perhaps most importantly, Maria, David, Emily, and Adam's efforts spark a sense

of hope and optimism in the hearts of their fellow residents. Through their dedication

and perseverance, they demonstrate that even in the face of adversity, positive

change is possible, and that together, they have the power to shape the future of their

community for the better.

As they reflect on how far they've come and the challenges they've overcome, Maria,

David, Emily, and Adam are filled with a renewed sense of purpose and

determination. They know that their journey is far from over, but they face the road

ahead with courage and conviction, knowing that they have planted the seeds of

hope that will continue to grow and flourish in the days and years to come.

Chapter 15: Nurturing Growth

In the aftermath of their recent successes, Maria, David, Emily, and Adam turn their

focus towards nurturing the growth of their projects and initiatives in Ramsey. With a

sense of optimism and determination, they work diligently to cultivate the seeds of

change they've planted and ensure that their impact continues to flourish.

At the sea life sanctuary, Adam and his team of volunteers devote themselves to the

care and conservation of the marine life housed within its walls. Through educational

programs and interactive exhibits, they strive to inspire a greater understanding and

appreciation for the ocean and its inhabitants, nurturing a sense of stewardship and

responsibility for the natural world.

Meanwhile, Emily expands her online storytelling platform, using her platform to

amplify the voices of marginalised communities and advocate for social justice

causes. Through powerful narratives and thought-provoking content, she sparks conversations and fosters empathy, nurturing a culture of compassion and

understanding in Ramsey and beyond.

David tends to the community garden with unwavering dedication, using it as a

space to teach others about sustainable agriculture and healthy living. Through

workshops and demonstrations, he shares his knowledge and expertise,

empowering residents to take control of their food sources and lead healthier, more

sustainable lives.

As their projects continue to grow and evolve, Maria, David, Emily, and Adam find

themselves buoyed by the support of their community and the progress they've

made together. Though challenges may arise along the way, they remain steadfast in

their commitment to creating positive change in Ramsey, nurturing the seeds of hope

they've planted and watched as they continue to flourish and thrive.

Chapter 16: Embracing Resilience

As the seasons change in Ramsey, Maria, David, Emily, and Adam find themselves

facing new challenges and opportunities with resilience and determination.

Embracing the lessons they've learned along their journey, they navigate the ups and

downs of life in their coastal town with grace and fortitude.

In the face of setbacks and obstacles, they draw strength from their shared sense of

purpose and the support of their community. Together, they weather the storms that

come their way, emerging stronger and more resilient with each passing day.

Maria leans on her faith and inner strength to navigate personal hardships, finding

solace in the beauty of nature and the support of her loved ones. David channels his

entrepreneurial spirit and creative energy into new ventures, seizing opportunities to

innovate and adapt in an ever-changing world.

Emily's passion for storytelling fuels her drive to create meaningful change, as she continues to use her platform to amplify marginalised voices and advocate for social

justice causes. Adam finds solace and purpose in his work at the sea life sanctuary,

where he witnesses the transformative power of nature and the resilience of the

ocean's creatures.

Together, Maria, David, Emily, and Adam embody the spirit of resilience that defines

their community, inspiring others to persevere in the face of adversity and embrace

the challenges that come their way. As they continue on their journey of growth and

transformation, they do so with courage, grace, and an unwavering belief in the

power of hope to light the way forward.

Chapter 17: Blossoms of Joy

In the heart of Ramsey, amidst the ebb and flow of daily life, Maria, David, Emily, and

Adam finds moments of pure joy that bloom like flowers in spring. Despite the

challenges they've faced, they cherish the simple pleasures and small victories that

bring light and warmth to their lives.

For Maria, it's the laughter of her children as they play in the garden and the quiet

moments of reflection she finds in the beauty of nature. David takes pride in the

growth of his community garden, where vibrant blossoms and bountiful harvests

bring colour and vitality to the town.

Emily finds joy in the connections she forms through her storytelling platform, as she

receives messages of gratitude and encouragement from readers near and far. And

for Adam, it's the wonder and awe of the visitors who flock to the sea life sanctuary,

their faces alight with fascination and curiosity.

Together, Maria, David, Emily, and Adam celebrate these moments of joy, recognizing them as beacons of light in the midst of life's challenges. They find strength and

resilience in the simple act of finding joy in the present moment, knowing that even in

the darkest times, there is always something to be grateful for and something to

smile about.

Chapter 18: Facing Fears

As life in Ramsey continues to unfold, Maria, David, Emily, and Adam confront their

fears head-on, finding courage in the face of uncertainty and adversity. Each one

grapples with their own inner demons and doubts, but they refuse to let fear hold

them back from pursuing their dreams and making a difference in their community.

Maria confronts her fear of failure as she takes on new challenges and ventures

outside of her comfort zone. With the support of her loved ones, she pushes past her

insecurities and embraces the unknown, finding strength in her resilience and

determination.

David wrestles with doubts about his abilities and the future of his community

garden, but he refuses to give in to despair. Drawing inspiration from the resilience of

the plants he tends to, he redoubles his efforts to nurture growth and cultivate hope

in the hearts of his neighbours.

Emily grapples with the fear of rejection as she continues to share her stories and

advocate for social change. Despite facing criticism and resistance, she remains

steadfast in her commitment to using her voice for good, finding courage in her

convictions and the support of her readers.

Adam confronts his fear of inadequacy as he navigates the challenges of running the

sea life sanctuary and caring for its inhabitants. Though doubts may linger, he finds

solace in the knowledge that every small step forward is a victory in itself, and that

with perseverance and determination, he can overcome any obstacle.

Together, Maria, David, Emily, and Adam learn that facing their fears is not about

being fearless, but about finding the strength to move forward in spite of them. As

they embrace the challenges that lie ahead, they discover a newfound sense of

courage and resilience that propels them ever closer to their dreams.

Chapter 19: Reaping Rewards

After months of hard work and dedication, Maria, David, Emily, and Adam begin to

reap the rewards of their efforts in Ramsey. Their perseverance and resilience have

paid off, as they witness the fruits of their labour manifesting in tangible ways

throughout the community.

Maria takes pride in the flourishing garden she has nurtured, as vibrant flowers and

bountiful crops fill the air with colour and fragrance. Her children frolic amidst the

greenery, their laughter echoing through the neighbourhood as they revel in the joy of

nature's abundance.

David's community garden has become a thriving hub of activity, as neighbours

come together to tend to the plants and share in the bounty of the harvest. The once

barren patch of land is now a vibrant oasis of life, teeming with vitality and energy.

Emily's storytelling platform has gained traction and recognition, reaching audiences far and wide with its powerful messages of hope and inspiration. Her stories have

sparked conversations and ignited change, leaving a lasting impact on those who

read them and empowering others to raise their voices for justice.

Adam's sea life sanctuary has become a beloved attraction in Ramsey, drawing

visitors from near and far to marvel at the wonders of the ocean. The aquarium

teems with life, its tanks filled with colourful fish and exotic creatures that captivate

the imagination and instil a sense of wonder in all who visit.

Together, Maria, David, Emily, and Adam revel in the rewards of their hard work and

dedication, knowing that they have made a positive impact on their community and

inspired others to join them in their mission. As they reflect on how far they've come,

they look forward to the journey ahead with renewed determination and hope.

Chapter 20: A New Chapter Begins

As one chapter of their lives comes to a close, Maria, David, Emily, and Adam stand

on the threshold of a new beginning in Ramsey. Their journey has been filled with

challenges and triumphs, setbacks and successes, but through it all, they have grown

stronger and more resilient, united by their shared vision for a better future.

With the dawn of a new day comes the promise of endless possibilities and

opportunities for growth and renewal. Maria, David, Emily, and Adam look ahead with

optimism and excitement, eager to embark on the next phase of their journey

together.

As they bid farewell to the past and embrace the future, they carry with them the

lessons they've learned and the memories they've shared. They know that the road

ahead may be uncertain and fraught with obstacles, but they also know that they are

stronger together, and that with courage, determination, and a steadfast belief in the power of hope, they can overcome anything that comes their way.

As they step into the unknown, Maria, David, Emily, and Adam do so with open hearts

and minds, ready to face whatever challenges and adventures lie ahead. For in the

journey of life, every ending is also a new beginning, and every obstacle is an

opportunity to grow, to learn, and to become the best versions of themselves.

With a sense of purpose and a spirit of resilience, they set forth into the world, ready

to write the next chapter of their story in Ramsey, where the seeds of change have

taken root and the promise of a brighter tomorrow awaits.

Chapter 21: Embracing Possibilities

As Maria, David, Emily, and Adam continue their journey in Ramsey, they find

themselves embracing the endless possibilities that lie before them. With each

passing day, they discover new opportunities for growth, connection, and

transformation, as they continue to nurture their dreams and aspirations.

In this chapter of their lives, Maria dives deeper into her passion for gardening,

exploring innovative techniques and sustainable practices to cultivate a thriving

ecosystem in her backyard. She shares her knowledge with her neighbours, inspiring

them to create their own green spaces and foster a sense of community through a

shared love of nature.

David expands his community garden project, collaborating with local schools and

organisations to educate children about the importance of environmental

stewardship and healthy eating. Together, they plant seeds of change that will flourish for generations to come, instilling a sense of responsibility and respect for

the planet in the hearts of young minds.

Emily's storytelling platform evolves into a powerful tool for social change, as she

amplifies the voices of marginalised communities and advocates for justice and

equality. Through her work, she sparks meaningful conversations and drives tangible

action, inspiring others to join the fight for a more just and equitable world.

Adam's sea life sanctuary continues to thrive, as he expands its offerings to include

educational programs, conservation initiatives, and interactive exhibits that engage

visitors of all ages. He fosters a deeper appreciation for the ocean and its

inhabitants, empowering others to take action to protect and preserve marine

ecosystems for future generations.

Together, Maria, David, Emily, and Adam embrace the possibilities that surround

them, knowing that the journey ahead will be filled with challenges and triumphs,

setbacks and successes. But they also know that with courage, resilience, and a

steadfast belief in the power of community, anything is possible. And so, they step

forward into the unknown, ready to embrace whatever the future may hold.

Chapter 22: Cultivating Connections

As Maria, David, Emily, and Adam continue to build their lives in Ramsey, they

prioritise nurturing the connections they've forged with their community. In this

chapter, they focus on deepening their relationships and fostering a sense of

belonging among their neighbours.

Maria opens her garden to the community, hosting regular gatherings and events

where neighbours come together to share stories, laughter, and the fruits of their

labour. Through these gatherings, she creates a space where bonds are

strengthened, friendships are formed, and a sense of kinship flourishes.

David expands his community garden project to include collaborative initiatives with

local businesses and organisations. Together, they work to beautify public spaces,

create urban green spaces, and promote sustainable living practices throughout the

town. Through these partnerships, David fosters a sense of pride and ownership among community members, empowering them to take an active role in shaping the

future of Ramsey.

Emily uses her storytelling platform to amplify the voices of underrepresented

groups within the community, sharing their stories of resilience, strength, and hope.

Through her work, she sparks conversations about diversity, inclusion, and social

justice, inspiring others to recognize the value of every voice and the power of

collective action.

Adam's sea life sanctuary becomes a hub for community engagement, hosting

educational workshops, volunteer programs, and outreach events that bring people

together to learn about marine conservation and stewardship. Through these

initiatives, Adam fosters a sense of responsibility and connection to the natural

world, empowering individuals to become advocates for ocean health.

Together, Maria, David, Emily, and Adam cultivate connections that enrich their lives

and strengthen the fabric of their community. As they work to build a more inclusive,

resilient, and compassionate society, they are reminded of the power of human

connection to overcome challenges and create positive change.

Chapter 23: Sowing Seeds of Change

In this pivotal chapter, Maria, David, Emily, and Adam continue to sow seeds of

change throughout Ramsey, inspiring others to join them in their mission to create a

more sustainable and inclusive community. As they work together to address

pressing issues and implement innovative solutions, they demonstrate the

transformative power of collective action.

Maria leads efforts to establish community gardens in underserved neighbourhoods,

providing residents with access to fresh, locally grown produce and fostering a

sense of pride and ownership in their surroundings. Through workshops and

educational programs, she empowers individuals to cultivate their own gardens,

promoting food security and self-sufficiency.

David collaborates with local businesses and government agencies to implement

green infrastructure projects aimed at mitigating the effects of climate change and enhancing the town's resilience to environmental hazards. From green roofs and rain

gardens to permeable pavement and bioswales, he champions sustainable design

practices that benefit both people and the planet.

Emily leverages her storytelling platform to raise awareness about social and

environmental issues facing the community, amplifying the voices of those most

affected and advocating for meaningful change. Through multimedia campaigns and

community forums, she sparks dialogue and inspires action, mobilising individuals to

stand up for justice and equity.

Adam expands his sea life sanctuary to include interactive exhibits and educational

programs focused on marine conservation and ocean literacy. By engaging visitors

of all ages in hands-on learning experiences, he instils a sense of responsibility and

stewardship for the ocean, fostering a new generation of environmental leaders.

Together, Maria, David, Emily, and Adam demonstrate the power of collaboration and

community engagement in driving positive change. Through their collective efforts,

they sow seeds of hope and resilience that take root and flourish, transforming

Ramsey into a beacon of sustainability, inclusion, and opportunity for all.

Chapter 24: Harvesting Hope

As the seasons change in Ramsey, Maria, David, Emily, and Adam witness the fruits

of their labour as they harvest hope and resilience throughout their community. In

this chapter, they reflect on their journey and celebrate the progress they've made in

creating a more sustainable, inclusive, and vibrant place to call home.

Maria's community gardens are thriving, providing an abundance of fresh produce to

residents and fostering a sense of connection and belonging among neighbours.

Through her efforts, she has cultivated not only nourishing food but also a sense of

community pride and empowerment.

David's green infrastructure projects have transformed the town, reducing flood risk,

improving air and water quality, and creating green spaces for residents to enjoy. His

vision for a more resilient and sustainable future has become a reality, thanks to his

tireless advocacy and dedication.

Emily's storytelling campaigns have sparked meaningful conversations and inspired collective action on issues ranging from social justice to environmental

conservation. Her ability to amplify marginalised voices and mobilise community

members have helped to build a more inclusive and equitable society.

Adam's sea life sanctuary has become a beloved destination for locals and tourists

alike, offering immersive experiences that educate and inspire visitors about the

wonders of the ocean. Through his work, he has fostered a deeper appreciation for

marine life and empowered individuals to take action to protect our oceans for future

generations.

As Maria, David, Emily, and Adam gather with their friends and neighbours to

celebrate the harvest season, they are filled with gratitude for the journey they've

shared and the community they've built together. In the midst of challenges and

uncertainties, they find strength in their connections and hope for the future, knowing

that together, they can overcome any obstacle and continue to sow the seeds of

positive change in Ramsey and beyond.

Chapter 25: A New Beginning

As the sun sets on another day in Ramsey, Maria, David, Emily, and Adam look out at

the town they've come to love and the community they've helped to nurture. In this

final chapter, they reflect on the journey that brought them here and the lessons

they've learned along the way.

Though their paths were filled with challenges and obstacles, they persevered,

guided by their shared vision of a better future for themselves and their neighbours.

Through their resilience, determination, and unwavering belief in the power of

community, they've transformed Ramsey into a place of hope, opportunity, and

Belonging. As they bid farewell to the old and welcome the new, Maria, David, Emily, and Adam

stand together, ready to embrace whatever the future may hold. With hearts full of

gratitude and optimism, they step forward into the next chapter of their lives,

knowing that the seeds of change they've planted will continue to grow and flourish for generations to come.

Series Title: The Impact Chronicles

Synopsis:

"The Impact Chronicles" is a series of interconnected stories that celebrate the

resilience, courage, and compassion of individuals striving to make a difference in

their communities and the world at large. Each instalment follows the journeys of

diverse characters as they navigate personal challenges, overcome obstacles, and

discover the transformative power of collective action.

In Book 1, "Seeds of Change: Stories of Hope and Resilience," readers are introduced

to the coastal town of Ramsey, where Maria, David, Emily, and Adam embark on a

quest to revitalise their community. Through their shared vision and unwavering

determination, they plant the seeds of change that inspire others to join them in their

mission to create a better future.

Book 2, "Roots of Resilience: Nurturing Change," delves deeper into the lives of the

residents of Ramsey as they confront economic hardships, environmental threats,

and personal struggles. Despite the odds, they draw strength from their roots and

work together to cultivate resilience, fostering a sense of belonging and

empowerment in their community.

In Book 3, "Echoes of Change: Shadows of the Past," Ramsey faces a new challenge when a devastating storm tests the town's resilience. As old wounds resurface and

tensions rise, the residents must confront the shadows of the past and find the

courage to rebuild and heal together, forging stronger bonds and deeper connections

in the process.

Book 4, "Seeds of Renewal: Love's Everlasting Bloom," shifts focus to Emily and

Adam as they navigate the complexities of love, loss, and renewal. Through their

journey, they discover that love has the power to heal wounds, ignite passions, and

inspire transformation, reminding them of the enduring hope that lies within each

new beginning.

Through its heartfelt narratives and compelling characters, "The Impact Chronicles"

explores the universal themes of compassion, resilience, and the profound impact of

small acts of kindness and courage. It serves as a testament to the indomitable

human spirit and the infinite possibilities that arise when individuals come together

to create positive change in the world.

Book 1

Title: Seeds of Change: A Journey to Ramsey

Summary:

In the first instalment of the "Seeds of Change" series, we follow the interconnected

stories of four individuals – Maria, David, Emily, and Adam – as they embark on a

journey to the coastal town of Ramsey in search of new beginnings.

Maria, a seasoned activist, arrives in Ramsey with a vision of creating community

gardens to promote food security and social cohesion. David, an environmental

engineer, sees Ramsey as an opportunity to implement green infrastructure projects

that will mitigate the effects of climate change and enhance the town's resilience.

Emily, a digital influencer, finds herself drawn to Ramsey's picturesque landscapes

and vibrant community spirit. With her online platform, she seeks to raise awareness

about local issues and inspire others to take action.

Adam, a marine biologist, is captivated by Ramsey's rich marine biodiversity and

sees potential in establishing a sea life sanctuary and tropical aquarium to educate

and engage visitors.

As these four individuals settle into Ramsey, they encounter challenges and setbacks

but also discover the power of community, resilience, and hope. Together, they plant

the seeds of change that will transform Ramsey into a beacon of sustainability, compassion, and renewal.

Through their journeys of self-discovery and collective action, Maria, David, Emily,

and Adam demonstrate that even in the face of adversity, ordinary individuals can

make an extraordinary impact when they come together with a shared purpose.

Let's go back to the beginning all those years ago.

Don't miss out!

Visit the website below and you can sign up to receive emails whenever Paul Smith publishes a new book. There's no charge and no obligation.

https://books2read.com/r/B-A-UCAEB-BUVXC

BOOKS 2 READ

Connecting independent readers to independent writers.

Also by Paul Smith

The Impact Chronicles
Seeds of Change: A Journey to Ramsey
Roots of Resilience: Nurturing Change
Roots of Resilience: Nurturing Change
Rising Tide: The Rebirth of Ramsey
Seeds of Renewal: Love's Everlasting Bloom

Watch for more at wix.pbsmith17@wix.com.

About the Author

Paul smith Artist, Aurthor & Designer. Island resident since 1999
Read more at wix.pbsmith17@wix.com.